A
Prophetic Call
for
NATIONAL
SHIFTING

AN UNDERSTANDING OF THE TIMES AND
SEASONS AND TAKING THE NECESSARY
ACTIONS TO SEIZE THEM

DAVID SAA FATORMA, JR.

A Prophetic Call for National Shifting

ISBN: 979-8-88898-066-8 - *Paperback*
ISBN: 979-8-88898-067-5 - *Hardcover*
ISBN: 979-8-88898-068-2 - *Ebook*

Cover design by Believe Stanley.

Published in Racine, Wisconsin by First Word, an imprint of Honor Books.

This book is dedicated, first and foremost, to the Almighty God, who is the source of the revelation contained in this book. We have reached this far solely by His grace, and for this, I am grateful.

I also want to dedicate this book to my dearest family; my wife, Veronica, whose encouragement and support fired me up to complete this project in a relatively short period of time; our children, Agnes, Christine, Davidnica, Olivia, and Christopher, who are so dear to me.

Finally, I dedicate this book to the children of God in my dear country, Liberia, Africa, and our global village, for whom this revelation is made readily available and is supposed to be the shifting agents.

Table of Contents

ACKNOWLEDGEMENTS

I acknowledge my dear friend and brother, who I have known for 24 years; Eusebio Jaimes Islas, a humble servant of God whom the Lord used in bringing the confirmational revelation for this book; a situation that pulled the trigger and got the project off the ground in a spur of the moment. Thanks, Eusebio. You are truly a brother, and this couldn't have been accomplished without you obeying God and traveling thousands of miles from the US, and spending thousands of dollars to bring confirmation.

I also acknowledge my dear friends and kingdom partners who had the privilege to read this book upfront and brought further confirmations, corrections, endorsements, encouragements, and all kinds of help. Words cannot express my gratitude to you.

Pastor Fatorma has heard from the Holy Spirit in writing this book. He has a remarkable understanding of what God is doing in Liberia and in the church. God is a God of seasons and Pastor Fatorma reveals in this book how important it is for us to understand God's seasons. God is calling nations and His church to shift. I encourage everyone to read this book because it will help us to embrace God's shifting.

Bishop Michael Thomas,

Good Shepherds Fellowship International, Inc.

I have read this book with enthusiasm, and I daresay that David speaks mainly to political leadership across the African continent with focus on Liberia. However, as a business person, this shifting is necessary and critical not only in the political arena, but in all forms of leadership. We need this shifting in business, in the family, in the church, and in all aspects of society. A must-read for anyone who believes God has empowered them to participate in choosing leaders.

Thanks, David, for being obedient. You have laid bare God's heart for African political leadership selection which is on the shoulders of every believer. I would encourage all to read this, and by this, we can shape the direction of our politics and business in Africa.

Stenford Masimba Chimwara,

Chairman, Christian Business Men Connection Intl. Africa

I have known Pastor David Fatorma for some years now and have always admired his heart and passion for Liberia. It is evident in this book that God is speaking. I recall when I first arrived to Liberia five years ago seeing the remnants of the war — buildings destroyed, extreme poverty, and oppression in a land that was once thriving. The Lord spoke to me and said He will restore Liberia and to tell His daughter that He has not forsaken her.

I believe that the time of restoration is coming for Liberia to shake off the things of the past, stop selling her inheritance for a cup of soup, and rise up in unity and rebuild. The time is truly now as Pastor David Fatorma has clearly depicted in this book.

Grab hold of the season and move forward.

Trecie Bolton,

Empowered to Restore Ministries International

The principle of leadership by inspiration is to bring potential leaders up to your level. I am so proud to have known Pastor David S. Fatorma since his days of training at the Liberia Christian College. He is a refined young man with great potential for advancing kingdom ideals in our nation. I read through the pages of this book and his concept of "National Shifting" is profound. How we need such a profound critical kingdom voice in this electioneering year in our nation! The spiritual problem of this nation is the doctrine of "instant gratification." The greatest and desperate need today for every nation is not a greater number of intelligent people, or gifted people, but for "deep people." "Superficiality is the curse of this age." Pastor Fatorma makes it simple in this book! I recommend this book to every leader.

Dr. Jackson G. Weah,

Resident Bishop,

Hope Renewal Ministries International

Pastor David Fatorma is a living testimony of a genuine minister and a credible ministry. His diligence and contagious passion to see national transformation through the preaching of the Gospel are evident. Some of his passion for national transformation is captured in the pages of this book. It reveals the yearning of a preacher for the progress of his country. It is authentic.

G Thomas Dowie,

Kingdom Restoration Ministries

This book emphasizes the importance of God's standards for national leadership. It highlights the need for leaders to have strong character, experience, and charisma. The author argues that national leadership is a critical and delicate area that requires serious attention from all of us.

The book also emphasizes the need for leaders to be gifted and have leadership abilities to perform exceedingly well. One of the book's strong points is its emphasis on the importance of character in national leadership. Brother David argues that leaders must have a strong moral compass and be guided by principles, protocols, and order.

This book also highlights the need for leaders to have experience and processing to fulfill the call of God on their lives. This is an important point as it emphasizes the need for leaders to have a track record of success and a deep understanding of the challenges they will face.

Another strong point of the book is its emphasis on the need for leaders to have charisma. The author argues that charisma is a personal quality or power that makes an individual capable of influencing or inspiring larger numbers of people. The book also highlights the importance of gifted leaders who are known by their fruits. This is an important point as it emphasizes the need for leaders to have the ability to lead and inspire others to achieve great things.

Overall, the book provides a compelling argument for the importance of God's standards for national leadership. It emphasizes the need for leaders to have strong character, experience, and charisma. The book also highlights the importance of gifted leaders who are known by their fruits. These are all important points that should be taken into consideration when choosing leaders for our nations.

H.M.S.,

Dr. Prince Maurice Parker

Professor of Old Testament History and Exegesis

Assemblies of God Theological Seminary

Assemblies of God of Spain

La Carlota, Córdoba, Spain

I have had the privilege of partnering in ministry with Pastor David Fatorma since 2007. Over these 16 years, I have been able to get to know David and his family and the ministry well. I have found him to be a man of passion and gift, but most of all integrity. I commend him for the bravery it has taken to write this book, and I pray it will be received as the prophetic challenge and exhortation that it is. David has a genuine love for Jesus Christ and a tremendous heart for Liberia and I commend him and this vital message to you in this critical hour.

John C. Lalgee

President

One Church Ministries

Foreword

I t was early morning on June 12, 2022, when I was awakened by a dream that I was in Liberia, West Africa. It has been almost 22 years since I left the country after spending a little over 2 years as a missionary. I was there from 1998 till the spring of 2000 during the civil war. I checked the clock; it was 4:00 AM Eastern Time here in my home in Pennsylvania. I remembered that I had a couple of missed calls from my friend, Pastor David, from Liberia.

Since I could not sleep any longer, I went to my computer to check the local time in Monrovia, Liberia, and it was 8:00 AM. So, I decided to finally return those missed calls. During our phone conversation, I asked the common question: "Sorry, I missed your calls; what can I do for you, brother?" On the other side of the phone, I heard something like this; "Man, you need to come to Liberia! You need to come and see what the Lord is doing in my country!" At this point, he had gotten my full attention because, for a long time, I had been praying for Liberia and the Lord had been speaking to me on some of the things He wanted to do in the nation. I was excited!

As I prepared for the trip to Liberia in response to Pastor David's invitation to minister in the multiple churches he has established around the country, I asked the Lord what He wanted me to speak about while in Liberia. As I was preparing the topics, one word that kept coming to me was resurrection.

I did a quick review of the history of the country, and I realized that just 3 months from that point would be exactly 43 years since problems started in the country when Master Sargent Samuel K.

Doe assassinated President William Tolbert on April 12, 1980. And from a biblical perspective, the number 40 means: trial, testing, and new beginning.

In this book, you will find scriptural references that speak to the significance of the number 40; a prophetic period of testing, trials, and new beginnings.

I am intrigued by the fact that when I shared with Pastor David the revelation that the Lord gave me for the nation, I was informed that it was indeed a confirmation because the Lord had already laid on Pastor David's heart a similar revelation for the shifting if you like resurrection, of the nation during this prophetic season as he had earlier addressed the Liberian senate and the nation on the urgent need for national shifting.

I am even more amazed that just a couple of months after this confirmation came to the nation of Liberia, we are talking about having a book available to us in a very short period that details the resurrection or shifting of this nation and other nations in their season of shifting.

Can the Almighty resurrect a nation from the rubble of war and struggle to a nation that will accomplish God's calling and purpose? Can God Almighty bring back to life a nation where its people lost their ability to dream for a better future for their children because of the constant instabilities?

Yes, we believe God can do it!

As I highly recommend this book, which is a true revelation from God for the shifting of nations, I pray that you will read it, experience your own shifting, and discover your own purpose by answering this call. By doing so, we will move toward the real transformation and change that we desperately need.

Pastor Eusebio Jaimes

Introduction

In June 2022, I was invited by the Liberian Senate as a guest speaker. When I received the invitation, I asked the Lord to give me a word for them and the nation, and the Lord directed me to speak on the theme: *An Urgent Call for National Shifting.*

Several months after bringing a prophetic word to the Liberian Senate and the nation on the need for urgent national shifting, we recently hosted a man of God from the US whom I have known for over 24 years, who brought a similar prophetic revelation for our country. Let us take a look at who he is and exactly what he also brought that triggered the writing of this book.

In the late 1990s, while in Bible College working on my Bachelors in Theology at the Liberia Christian College, I met a friend who was also my Spanish instructor called Eusebio Jaimes Islas, commonly known as Chebo.

Chebo is a Mexican who had come to Liberia as a missionary to the African Christian Fellowship International (ACFI); the ministry that pioneered the Liberia Christian College. Chebo took a part-time job as a Spanish instructor at the newly established college. I was a good French student, but I took advantage of the Spanish class, which helped me to learn a few Spanish words and sentences, which have been helpful to my ministry today.

After a couple of years, Chebo traveled to the US, where he got married and established his family.

In my many travels to the US since 2007, I have consistently visited my friend, Chebo, who lives in Pennsylvania. While there, we spend quality time praying and talking about my dear country, Liberia. Chebo's heart for Liberia is gold, and we have always talked about the day he would return to Liberia for short-term missionary work.

Finally, that wish came to fruition when we received him, his son, Luis, his niece, Erica from Mexico, and Erica's son Julio, as well as two other young men, Darron and Noah both from the US also, who were here with us in January 2023, at Light Streams Chapel for a couple of weeks serving in missions.

Immediately upon arrival, Chebo shared with me a revelation that God had given him for the nation. He told me that the Lord had laid on his heart to speak to our nation of the times and seasons we are currently in. Like the children of Issachar who understood the times and seasons and knew exactly what to do, I was immediately reminded of what the Lord laid on my heart several months ago and have chosen to champion and trumpet this message across the nation, especially in a critical election year. Indeed, there could be no better time to have received such a powerful revelation.

We are reminded that from 1980 to 2020, we hit the 40th season as a nation. Moving forward, I will bring you a synopsis of the history that highlights how our nation was founded, laying the foundation for our discourse.

1980 to 2020 is a period of forty long years during which a lot of things happened that have caused the nation to go into chaos taking the lives of tens of thousands of people. An estimated 250,000 people lost their lives in a nation of 5 million people, especially during the civil war.

The revelation speaks about the shifting that occurs in the lives of individuals, families, and nations after every forty years, and truly so, for Liberia.

Based on this revelation, the Lord has laid on my heart to speak to the nation about a prophetic call for national shifting, an understanding of the times and seasons, and taking the necessary actions to redeem the nation and put it back on the right trajectory in accordance with its God-given purpose.

While I wrote this book in an election year of our country, a year that marks 43 years of the season we are speaking of, let me make it clear that this book is nonpolitical, and it is not intended to benefit any politician or a political institution as my true intent is to bring the mind of God to this nation and other nations of the world especially those in their own shifting season.

It may interest you to know that in the process of writing this book, we also hosted a friend from Zimbabwe who spent some time with us at church and in our home. During her visit to our home, I shared this project with her, and when she heard the book title and especially the theme of the 40th season, she was astonished as she mentioned to me that her country, Zimbabwe, is also in a season of shifting. This is because they attained their independence in 1980 and that country has also been through a lot in the last four decades.

Besides these two countries, Africa as a whole and many countries around the world are sensing the cloud of shifting, and it's high time we grabbed this revelation and be like the children of Issachar who understood the times and knew what to do.

"And of the children of Issachar, which were men that had an understanding of the times, to know what Israel ought to do."

1 CHRONICLES 12:32A

It is my hope that you will find this book interesting to read as we strive to reach as many people as possible, especially those who are the children of Light and are supposed to be the vehicle that will trigger the necessary shifting that is badly needed to restore our nation and the nations of the world especially those in their own season of shifting.

CHAPTER ONE

A Synopsis of the Nation's History

A s we move forward on this project to bring God's prophetic revelation regarding the nation, it is important that we take a look at the history of the nation. This is to give us a clear picture of how it all started, the major events since then, and where we are currently. This will provide us with a better understanding of the necessity for national shifting and restoration.

The history of Liberia began with the arrival of Portuguese traders in the mid-1400s and the rise of the trans-Atlantic trade. Coastal groups traded several goods with Europeans, but the area became known as the Grain Coast because of its rich supply of malagueta pepper grains.

In 1816, the future of Liberia changed dramatically due to the formation of the American Colonization Society (ACS) in the United States. Looking for a place to re-settle free-born Black Americans and formerly enslaved people, the ACS chose the Grain Coast. In 1822, the ACS founded Liberia as a colony of the United States of America. Over the next few decades, 19,900 Black American men and women migrated to the colony.

On July 26, 1847, Liberia declared its independence from America. Interestingly, the United States refused to acknowledge Liberia's independence until 1862, when the U.S. government ended the practice of enslavement during the American Civil War.

The oft-stated claim that after the Scramble for Africa, Liberia was one of two African states to remain independent is misleading because the indigenous African societies had little economic or political power in the new republic.

Instead, all powers were concentrated in the hands of the African-American settlers and their descendants, known as Americo-Liberians. In 1931, an international commission revealed that several prominent Americo-Liberians had enslaved indigenous people.

The Americo-Liberians constituted less than 2 percent of Liberia's population, but in the 19th and early 20th centuries, they made up nearly 100 percent of qualified voters. For over 100 years, from its formation in the 1860s until 1980, the Americo-Liberian True Whig Party dominated Liberian politics in what was essentially a minority-ruled one-party state.

Though they were Black, the Americo-Liberians created a cultural divide. From the day they arrived, they set about establishing an American, rather than African, culture. They spoke English, dressed like Americans, built southern plantation-style homes, ate American foods, practiced Christianity, and lived in monogamous relationships. They modeled the Liberian government after that of the United States.

On April 12, 1980, Master Sgt. Samuel K. Doe and less than 20 soldiers overthrew the Americo-Liberian president, William R. Tolbert Jr., who was subsequently murdered in cold blood in his official residence, the Executive Mansion. Thirteen of some of his most senior government officials were also killed by a firing squad after an extra-judicial process that found them guilty of rampant corruption.

The Liberian people celebrated the coup d'état as liberation from Americo-Liberian domination. However, Doe's dictatorial government proved no better for Liberians than its predecessor. After a coup attempt against him in 1985 failed, Doe responded with brutal atrocities against suspected conspirators and their followers.

The United States, however, had long used Liberia as an important base of operations in Africa, and during the Cold War, the U.S. provided millions of dollars in aid that helped prop up Doe's increasingly unpopular regime.

CIVIL WARS

In 1989, a former Americo-Liberian official, Charles Taylor invaded Liberia with his National Patriotic Front. Backed by Libya, Burkina Faso, and the Ivory Coast, Taylor soon controlled much of the eastern part of Liberia. Doe was assassinated in 1990, and for the next five years, Liberia was divided among competing warlords who made millions exporting the country's resources to foreign buyers. The war was so brutal that some of the most heinous crimes against humanity were committed during that period and it took the lives of an estimated 250,000 persons.

After nearly 14 years of civil war, a peace accord was signed by various warring factions in 2003, which brought lasting peace to the country. The agreement saw Charles Taylor, former warlord and president, vacate the country for the neighboring West African state, Nigeria.

Not only does this unique history give a clear picture of the inception of the nation, but also projects the need to shift. More importantly, it gives a clue of our purpose as a nation. Meanwhile, in the next chapter, we will unravel the original purpose for the establishment of Liberia.

CHAPTER TWO

A Discovery of National Purpose

In this chapter, our goal is to unravel our purpose as a nation, and it could not have come at a better time than when we have just learned the history of the nation. This is very important because a purpose-driven nation thrives, but one without purpose struggles; and that's the case with Liberia. We have lost our purpose, and it is high time we go back to God's original intent for the founding of Liberia.

It is recorded in history that when the founding fathers who were in search of freedom landed on the shores of Liberia, their intent for coming was to find freedom from slavery, restrictions, and limitations. They wanted to be in a place where freedom abounds.

Liberia's national motto is: "The love of liberty brought us here." These words are seen on our national seal and some banknotes. In fact, the word, Liberia, means, "land of the free." The name itself tells you that the people who founded the nation were in search of freedom.

My question today is: "Yes, we are supposedly an independent and free nation but are we truly politically independent as a nation, or do we have western powers dictating to us because of our immaturity? Even though we are a country blessed with abundant natural resources and a very small population of under 6 million, are we truly economically independent or free?

How can we claim to be independent when western powers harvest our natural resources, but if managed properly, these resources could transform our country into a thriving economy and get our people out of the dungeon of poverty?

2 Corinthians 3:17b indicates that, *"Where the Spirit of the Lord is, there is freedom."* True freedom is realized when God is in it. History reveals that when the founding fathers arrived on this nation's shores, Africa was a completely dark continent where the indigenous people worshipped idols, rivers, mountains, and ancestral spirits. However, it will interest you to know that as the settlers came, they brought with them the Gospel.

Consequently, the church was established, and Liberia became that shining star bringing light to the dark continent of Africa. I remember when I was in elementary school back in the day. I learned the meaning of our national flag. The blue field on the upper left corner of the flag represents the dark continent of Africa, and the star represents Liberia which brings light to a dark continent. Originally, we lived up to that purpose as Liberia became that country where the Gospel prospered.

Today, can we say that we are still the nation that is a shining example on the hilltop? Are we still that nation in Africa that brings spiritual light to other African nations that are struggling spiritually?

The truth is that the religious community (the Church) has been compromised to a large extent, so much so that we do not have the moral standing to question some of the things that happen in the dark. It is high time we shift and go back to our original purpose.

We can also conclude that the nation was founded as a beacon of hope for people whose lives were shattered and who lived in hopelessness. Liberia became the beacon of hope for not just those who were hopeless as a result of painful years of slavery and inhumane treatment from slave masters in the United States of America but also for the indigenous Liberians who, even though lived a free life prior to the coming of the settlers, weren't truly free without Christ as freedom without God is not freedom at all. When people are involved with ancestral and idol worship, that absolutely is hopelessness.

The nation became a beacon of hope for Africa as Christianity spread across the nation. As we stated earlier, the establishment of evangelistic missions across the country, such as the Eternal Love Winning Africa (ELWA) mission through its radio broadcasts reached across Africa with the message of hope that saw many people receive hope in Jesus Christ.

It is important to note that discovering our true purpose as a nation will put us back on the right trajectory.

The actualization of true freedom and hope is very critical to the forward march of our nation. This cannot be achieved if we do not understand the times and seasons and act accordingly.

Because we are a very compliant nation, we have endured a lot of pains and troubles over the years as wicked leaders and politicians took advantage of our passive nature, thereby keeping the people in wars, economic bondage, and spiritual darkness based on their actions. It is high time the nation goes back to its roots, and we shall truly be freed.

CHAPTER THREE

We Are The Source of Our Problems

It is often said that "a problem shared is a problem half solved". However, I would like to add to this by saying that "a problem discovered is a problem nearly solved". Before a problem is shared, it has to be discovered. That is why we say, "discovery brings recovery".

I am saying all of this to make the point that Liberia's problems did not start today. They started almost when the nation was birthed. However, the 1980 military coup became the symbol of the nation's dilemma, as we will soon discover when we talk about times and seasons in the next chapter.

Meanwhile, for now, this chapter focuses on unraveling the problems that have held us down all this while. Without any shadow of doubt, we are the source of our problems. Let us take a look at some of the problems that have caused the misery and troubles for this country and many other nations.

SYNCRETISM

To begin with, it is important to look at the spiritual root of our problems. Once the spirituality is handled, the physical will succumb. Syncretism is one of the main sources of our problems as a nation, especially in our national leadership. The vast majority of our past and present leaders practice syncretism. Syncretism is basically the practice of multiple religions.

A common practice of syncretism in our nation, mainly in our national leadership, is the blending of Christianity, freemasonry, and traditional worship. Sometimes, the same leaders who claim to be Christians also engage in Islamic worship. This hypocritical act of worship, particularly among national leaders who are the face of the nation, invokes the curse of God. From time to time, we discover in Scripture that every time the children of God partook of the worship of other gods, there were dire consequences. In fact, many lost their lives in the process as they experienced the wrath of God.

Let us look at some biblical examples of the practice of syncretism and the consequences thereof. God warns against this practice:

> *"I am the Lord your God who brought you out of Egypt, out of the land of slavery. You shall have no other gods before me. You shall not make for yourself as image in the form of anything in heaven above or on the earth beneath or in the waters below.*

You shall not bow down to them or worship them; for I, the Lord your God, am a jealous God, punishing the children for the sin of the parents to the third and fourth generation of those who hate me."

EXODUS 20:2-5 NIV

These Scriptures clearly manifest how much God hates and warns against syncretism. At some point, Joshua, the servant of God, challenged the Israelites in their hypocrisy when he said this:

"But if serving the Lord seems undesirable to you, then choose for yourselves this day whom you will serve, whether the gods your ancestors served beyond the Euphrates or the gods of the Amorites in whose land you are living. But as for me and my household, we will serve the Lord."

JOSHUA 24:15 NIV

I have come to realize that two factors inform the practice of syncretism, particularly among national leaders; the quest for political and financial power, as it is believed that some of these religions or secret societies are the gateway to attaining political and economic power. Secondly, it is a means of appeasing a political base to attain numerical strength.

Because success in attaining political power depends on one's numerical strength, politicians will go to any length to appease a certain base, even if it means compromising their faith. If you are a Christian, be a devout and a good Christian; in fact, not only because God is pleased and blesses you when you do so, but you also earn the respect of folks from other religions. You are seen as a faithful and devout worshipper, not a hypocrite who cannot be trusted.

SHEDDING OF INNOCENT BLOOD/RITUAL KILLINGS

Shedding innocent blood and ritual killings are another of Liberia's problems.. These are common practices for the attainment of wealth and political power. As we highlighted earlier in the history of the nation, while it is true that the shedding of blood is an age-old problem, in 1980, there was a mass execution of national leaders in Liberia. Whether or not they went through a proper judicial trial, the fact that they represented the nation and such a horrible act took place was the invocation of God's curse and the inception of major crises.

God said this to Cain when he killed his brother due to envy:

"The Lord said, what have you done? Listen! Your brother's blood cries out to me from the ground."

GENESIS 4:10 NIV

Blood, especially innocent blood, is so powerful that it cries out to God. The blood of many innocent people has been crying out to God against the nation, and inasmuch as we may not be individually guilty of such atrocities, we suffer a collateral damage when the nation is cursed as a result of the consistent wickedness of our brethren.

Earlier, we talked about ritual killings; a common practice amongst wicked politicians and wealth-hungry people. When politicians who seek political power go to witch doctors for help in their quest to attain power, in most cases, they are told to bring human parts and fresh blood.

Meanwhile, wicked and gullible politicians will go all out to do as requested, and scores of our innocent brothers, sisters, and children have fallen prey to this devilish act.

The same applies to those who want to get rich at all costs. They can do anything to accomplish their aim, even if it means taking the lives of their own family members.

Let's take a look at what God says in His Word about murder:

"Do this so that innocent blood will not be in your land, which the Lord your God is giving you as your inheritance, and so that you will not be guilty of blood shed."

DEUTERONOMY 19:10 NIV

Here, God clearly indicates that bloodshed should not be allowed in the land as He goes further by intimating that there is collective guilt that comes when this happens. As I said earlier, as a nation, we have suffered the curse of shedding innocent blood in the land over the years, and that's why this book is written to blow the trumpet and sound the alarm.

DISHONESTY AND CORRUPTION

The problem of dishonesty and corruption can never be overemphasized as these are the reasons the nation languishes in abject poverty, leaving its people at the mercy of foreigners who dictate the day-to-day running of our national economy.

Dishonesty is a problem that has plagued our society in every sector, both private and public. Normally, once the topic of corruption is mentioned, it is discussed in the public sector context. However, dishonesty and corruption are problems that affect every aspect of our society ranging from the family, the church, schools, businesses or companies, hospitals and clinics, and, of course, government.

Let's take a look at what Scripture says about corruption:

"They have sunk deep into corruption, as in the days of Gibeah. God will remember them for their wickedness and punish them for their sins."

HOSEA 9:9 NIV

This passage of Scripture clearly highlights the extent to which a people can sink into corruption. In every sector of our society, leaders have sunk into corruption and dishonesty. The result thereof is abject poverty. Because family is the foundational pillar of society, as a father, I regularly remind my children of their moral responsibility. For example, if Mom, Dad, or any person gives you money to go down the street and buy something and change is left, you are under a moral obligation to return the full change.

In a family where morality is swept under the carpet, corruption thrives and the same attitude is brought to the public sector. This leads to the breakdown of morality in society, so in most instances, dishonesty and corruption have become the norm.

One thing that is clear in Hosea 9:9b is that God remembers and punishes corruption: *"God will remember their wickedness and punish them for their sins."*

I have seen in my short time on earth a few leaders rise to power and wealth and use the wealth of the nation to enrich themselves. They have siphoned those resources to build massive buildings. After a short while, when they are no longer in power, the buildings lie in ruins as their children are incapable of maintaining them.

One of the things that I have also seen that makes us the source of our own problems is that many poor people ridicule leaders with moral character. They refer to people who serve in the public sector and don't steal public money to build a house, get a new car, or improve the livelihood of their family members as big fools. This attitude has influenced many public servants to capitalize on their opportunity and even steal, fearing that people will make fun of them for missing their opportunity once it is gone.

So, instead of holding our hired servants serving in government and other public sectors accountable, we hail them as smart when they steal, and ridicule them when they are honest. We are certainly the source of our own problems.

THE ESAU MENTALITY

One of the many problems that have kept us backward and in abject poverty as a nation is the problem of greed and instant gratification. This happens when people yield to momentary satisfaction, which is also called the "Esau mentality". Esau, Isaac's eldest son, and Jacob's older brother, also known as Edom, is remembered as the man who sold his birthright to satisfy his hunger and did not care about his future; a decision that haunted and affected him throughout his lifetime.

Let's take a look at exactly what the Scripture says about Esau's careless attitude:

"Once when Jacob was cooking some stew, Esau came in from

the open country, famished (extremely hungry). He said to Jacob, 'quick let me have some of that red stew! I am famished (extremely hungry) [that's why he is called Edom].'

Jacob replied, 'first sell me your birth right.' 'Look I am about to die' Esau said 'what good is the birthright to me?' But Jacob said 'swear to me first' So he swore an oath to him, selling his birthright to Jacob. Then Jacob gave Esau some bread and some lentil stew. He ate and drank, and then got up and left. So, Esau despised his birthright."

GENESIS 25:29-34 NIV

It is clearly seen in these passages of Scripture that Esau returned from the fields extremely hungry and met his brother, Jacob, preparing red stew and requested some of the stew from his brother.

Jacob, being a cunning younger brother, used that moment to his advantage and asked his elder brother to sell him his birthright as the firstborn brother. Listen to Esau's response: *"What good is the birthright to me?"*

At this point, Esau was starving, and all he was concerned about was filling his stomach, and boom; he openly declared to his younger brother his desire to trade his right as the eldest son to his father. This speaks to the power of words. Isaac may not have heard this conversation, but words are very powerful, and they manifest in the fullness of time.

The rest of the story of Jacob and Esau shows a sad end for Esau, a decision he regretted for the rest of his life as Jacob received the blessing of the elder brother from their father, Isaac.

In this nation, we have many of our compatriots who are carriers of the Esau mentality, particularly the younger generation. Interestingly, because life expectancy is low here, the number of young people who call the shots in every circle of our elections is very high.

This generation is very selfish, shortsighted, and self-centered. Due to the harsh and unfavorable economic conditions created by the same wicked politicians, every election year, they sell their future, if you like, sacrifice their future, on the altar of a pittance, beer or stout, a T-shirt, etc. Sadly, we have heard these kinds of slogans: "You kill my pa, you kill my ma; I will vote for you." "You know book, you *na* (don't) know book; I will vote for you." "You steal any amount, as long as you built here, I will vote for you."

These people will go to any length to insult and, at some point, assault individuals who have an opposing political view.

You may have heard about the two kinds of thieves: the political thief and the ordinary thief.

The ordinary thief steals your money, your bag, your watch, and your jewelry, but the political thief steals your future, your career, your education, your health, and your business. The tragic reality is that the ordinary thief will choose whom to rob, but we the people, are the ones that choose the political thief to rob us because we vote for them!

The ridiculous part is that we will fight and protect our belongings from the ordinary thief, but we fight one another to defend and protect the political thief. We fight one another to defend and protect those who are stealing our future, our careers, our jobs, our health, etc. Folks, we have a call on our hands to shift; I mean, to change the narrative and set the nation on the right trajectory.

There can be no better time for an earthquake of shifting that will shock the traditional and wicked politicians than now. The power is in your hands; act like the men of Issachar who understood the times and seasons and knew exactly what to do to facilitate a paradigm shift.

SYCOPHANCY AND FLATTERY

Let's take a quick look at a simple definition of sycophant; "Someone who praises powerful or rich people in a way that is not sincere, usually in order to get some advantage from them."

From this simple definition, we can deduce that sycophancy is common around powerful people, particularly politicians and wealthy people in society. This is rife in our society today.

> *"Woe to those who call evil good and good evil. Who put darkness for light and light for darkness, who put bitter for sweet and sweet for bitter."*
>
> ISAIAH 5:20 NIV

This verse of Scripture clearly indicates the hypocrisy and deceit in sycophants and flatterers in every aspect of our society. People will see good and call it evil and call evil, good; light, darkness; darkness, light; sweet, bitter; and bitter, sweet. Most times, it is because they are connected to an individual or organization that they are loyal to, and, of course, without a shadow of a doubt, it is blind loyalty for the enhancement of their own selfish interest with total disregard to the welfare of society.

Meanwhile, God promises a curse for those involved in such practices, which results in society being a dangerous place, engulfed by poverty and injustice. When people in power turn a blind eye to the truth and play sycophancy and flattery, the society is subject to collapse!

It is important to note that most people have resorted to syco-phancy and flattery because of their selfish interests, instant gratification, and momentary happiness. This kind of deceit, found especially in the political arena, is killing the nation and keeping us in a vicious cycle. I have seen people get so sycophantic that they insult and sometimes assault good people who speak the truth that is not in their interest.

In 1 Kings 22, we are told of the 400 sycophantic prophets who were preserved by King Ahab and Queen Jezebel, who served as leaders of the northern Kingdom of Israel during a time of much evil in the land. Listen to the narrative.

> "But Jehoshaphat also said to the king of Israel, 'first seek the counsel of the Lord.' So, the King of Israel brought together the prophets – about four hundred men – and asked them, 'shall I go to war against Ramoth Gilead, or shall I refrain?' 'Go,' they answered, 'for the Lord will give it into the king's hand.' But Jehoshaphat asked 'is there no longer a prophet of the Lord here whom we can inquire of?' The king of Israel answered Jehoshaphat, 'There is still one prophet through whom we can inquire of the Lord, but I hate him because he never prophesies anything good about me, but always bad. He is Micaiah the son of Imlah."

1 KINGS 22:5-8 NIV

From this narrative, there was a pending battle between Israel and Syria over Ramoth Gilead; a place believed to be Israel's but was occupied by Syria. When King Jehoshaphat of Judah was on a visit to Israel, Ahab reminded Jehoshaphat about Ramoth Gilead. Ahab asked Jehoshaphat to join him in the battle to retake Ramoth Gilead. Jehoshaphat agreed but on condition to inquire of the Lord.

King Ahab quickly called 400 of his sycophantic prophets, and they instantly said they should go to battle and they would win. Jehoshaphat was a bit cynical about the prophecy and asked if there wasn't any other prophet in the land to confirm. The king replied that there was one Micaiah who was a prophet, but Ahab didn't hide his feelings by saying that he hated him because he had always brought him bad prophecy.

Imagine 400 false prophets versus one true prophet in biblical days. Since biblical days till now, how many sycophantic and false prophets do we not have in our pulpits, spewing falsehoods for politicians and the ordinary people? We can project millions of them everywhere.

The story of the naked emperor is a classic example of sycophancy and flattery that's killing our nations. The story is about a very vain emperor who placed much emphasis on flamboyancy and exterior trapping of success. At some point in his reign, he was approached by a fake clothing designer who promised him the best outfit ever; one that was invisible and that none had worn.

From the story, it was clear that the clothing designer aimed to make money off the emperor.

He, however, managed to convince the emperor, who was addicted to sycophancy and flattery, that his garment was invisible. Then came the day when emperors paraded and displayed their unique garments. The emperor paraded naked through the streets. However, a young child called out, "But he is naked," and the naked truth emerged. Some of his followers saw it for what it was; pure nonsense indeed. However, the emperor himself and those around him continued their foolish charade, and no one wanted to admit they couldn't see the garment.

In today's world, we sadly see a replica of this reality in our nations as national leaders surround themselves with cheering squads who will say to them things they want to hear as they continue in their misrule. What is even more astonishing is that some of those in the cheering squad are renowned men and women of God who are expected to stand for the truth and speak truth to power.

Sadly, they are unable to speak truth to power because they are in the pockets of our national leaders, with some serving in lucrative positions in government. The truth is that there is a time of reckoning, and very soon, your sycophancy and flattery will catch up with you.

CHAPTER FOUR

Understanding of the Times and Seasons

"And of the children of Issachar, which were men that had understanding of the times, to know what Israel ought to do."

1 CHRONICLES 12:32A NIV

I n this chapter, my goal is to present to you a revelation that triggered the writing of this book. This has to do with the times and seasons we are in as a nation and what needs to be done to initiate the country's shifting.

The children of Issachar were men who understood the times and seasons. Not only that, they also knew what to do. In our next chapter, we will certainly talk about the practicality of the times and seasons we are in, but for now, let's look at the times we are in.

In my introduction, I mentioned that in June 2022, I was invited as a guest speaker at the Liberian House of Senate. In my preparation, the Lord laid on my heart to speak on the theme: *An urgent call for national shifting*. The immediate response to that message was great. The senate *pro tempore* was grateful for the message and went further by asking another renowned senator to express appreciation on behalf of the senate to me for bringing God's prophetic word to them, and they promised to act accordingly.

The question as to whether it bore fruit is anyone's guess. However, one thing is certain; seeds were sown on that day, and that's why we are here blowing the trumpet further for the shifting of the nation.

As I mentioned earlier, in January 2023, I received a friend of 23 years, who I consider a prophet to the nation, with practically the same message.

The prophetic word speaks to the fact that, as a nation, we are in our shifting season after 40 years of testing, pain, and difficulty. It is time for a shift. From 1980 when our troubles began, which led to the brutal murder of a sitting president, his son, and 13 of his senior government officials, is a long stretch of 40 years.

This is a period in which we encountered one of the most devastating civil wars recorded in modern history that lasted for 14 years. Within that period, an estimated 250,000 lives were destroyed. Even after the civil war, our economy and infrastructure lie in ruins. Elected post-war leaders continued to suppress the vast majority of the people, keeping them in poverty and enriching themselves at the expense of the poor.

As a nation, we are at the crossroad, and our understanding of this season and acting upon it is very critical.

The number 40 is mentioned 146 or 149 times in Scripture

depending on the translation you use. The number 40 symbolizes a period of testing, trial, and triumph. This is seen practically throughout the Bible, where the number 40 is recorded.

Folks, based on our nation's history, we can surmise that as a nation from the 80s when hell broke loose and having experienced testing of times and trials, we are now in the season of triumph.

A SCRIPTURAL ANALYSIS OF THE SIGNIFICANCE OF THE NUMBER FORTY

Let us embark on a biblical survey and analyze the significance of the number 40 based on the above narratives. To begin with, let us look at what God said to Noah regarding destroying the earth:

> *"And God looked upon the earth and behold it was corrupt; for all flesh had corrupted the way upon the earth. And God said unto Noah the end of all flesh is come before me; the earth is filled with violence through them; and, behold, I will destroy them with the earth."*

GENESIS 6:12-13 KJV

Here, we see that God informed Noah about the pending destruction of the earth due to the wickedness and corruption that had permeated the earth. God did exactly what He promised to do. Noah was instructed to build an ark for him, his family and animals that would be spared them to start the new earth.

We see exactly how God plans to destroy the earth:

"For yet seven days, and I will cause it to rain upon the earth forty days and forty nights; and every living substance that I have made will I destroy from off the earth."

GENESIS 7:4 KJV

The planned destruction of the earth was already building up. Almighty God was ready to bring down judgment upon the earth by flood, which would last forty days and forty nights.

And it came to pass that as Noah completed the ark and got his family into it along with all the animals on the face of the earth, the rain began to fall and destroyed the earth's inhabitants.

Now, after forty days of heavy downpours of rain, came hope:

"And it came to pass at the end of forty days, that Noah opened the window of the ARK which he had made."

GENESIS 8:6 KJV

Noah had sent a raven out to check if the waters were dried up from off the earth. Later was a dove that came back with this encouraging sign:

"And the dove came in to him in the evening; and, lo, in her mouth was an olive leaf pluck off: so, Noah knew that the waters were abated from off the earth."

GENESIS 8:11 KJV

Hallelujah! After forty days and forty nights of destructive rain, finally, there was hope for a new earth. A new day had emerged!

We are told that when Moses clocked 40 years, even though

he lived in the palace of the Pharaoh of Egypt, Moses felt the need to embark on a mission to free his people, the Israelites, from the bondage of Egyptian slavery.

> *"And when he was full forty years old, it came into his heart to visit his brethren the children of Israel. And seeing one of them suffered wrong, he defended him, and avenged him that was oppressed, and smote the Egyptian."*
>
> ACTS 7:23-24 KJV

Meanwhile, after that encounter, Moses realized that the news of his killing of the Egyptian for an Israelite would have reached Pharaoh, and he fled to the desert of Midian where he spent another 40 years before receiving the call to return to Egypt for the deliverance mission.

> *"And when 40 years were expired, there appeared to him in the wilderness on Mount Sinai an angel of the Lord in the flame of fire in a bush."*
>
> ACTS 7:30 KJV

During that encounter, this is what God said to Moses:

> *"I have seen, I have seen the affliction of my people which is in Egypt, and I have heard their groaning, and am come, I will send thee into Egypt."*
>
> ACTS 7:34 KJV

After receiving the call to deliver his people from Egyptian bondage at 40, Moses fled for fear for his life as a result of killing an Egyptian for an Israelite. However, the fact is that he was running into a period of preparation and processing which took another 40 years.

After 40 years of a harsh life from royalty to poverty in the hot desert of Midian, where he became a shepherd, God called him to return to Egypt to lead the Israelites out of Egypt to the Promised Land.

At other times during their journey to the Promised Land, God asked Moses to go to Mount Sanai to receive the Ten Commandments; a composition of divine rules and oracles that would serve as a guide to the nation.

Here, once again, Moses spent 40 days and 40 nights. Let us take a look at what Scripture says:

"The Lord said to Moses, 'Come up to me on the mountain and stay here, and I will give you tablets of stone with the law and commandment I have written for their instruction.'

Then Moses set out with Joshua, his aide, and Moses went up on the mountain of God. He said to the elders, 'Wait here for us until we come back to you. Aaron and Hur are with you, and anyone involved in a dispute can go to them.'

When Moses went up to the mountain, the cloud covered it, and the glory of the Lord settled on Mount Sanai.

For six days the cloud covered the mountain, and on the seventh day the Lord called to Moses from within the cloud. To the Israelites the glory of the Lord looked like a consuming fire on top of the mountain. Then Moses entered the cloud as he went on up the mountain. And he stayed on the mountain 40 days and 40 nights."

EXODUS 24:12-18 KJV

In these passages of Scripture, we are told of the number 40 in Moses' ministry as God called him on the mountain for 40 days and 40 nights.

Meanwhile, in the New Testament as it is recorded, Jesus had a double experience of His own forty. To begin with, Jesus triumphed over one of the biggest temptations of his ministry immediately after fasting for 40 days and 40 nights.

Let us look at these passages of Scripture as revealed by Matthew:

"Then Jesus was led by the spirit into the wilderness to be tempted by the devil. After fasting forty days and forty nights, He was hungry. The tempter came to him and said, 'if you are the son of God, tell these stones to become bread.' Jesus answered, 'it is written: Man shall not live by bread alone, but on every word that comes from the mouth of God.'"

MATTHEW 4:1-4 NIV

The narrative in these passages clearly indicates that Jesus was tempted by the devil after he had fasted for forty days and forty nights, and yet he triumphantly overcame that temptation.

Another time in Jesus' ministry, we see the number forty playing out after His resurrection. Let's take a look at Dr. Luke's account:

"After His suffering, he presented himself to them and gave many convincing proofs that he was alive. He appeared to them over a period of forty days and spoke about the kingdom of God."

ACTS 1:3 NIV

While we differ with other religions on the way and the truth, and the truth remains that Jesus is the way, the truth, and the life. The spiritual significance of the mysterious number 40 cuts across the aisle in religions, cultures, and traditions. For example, this is what I found on the Islamic view of the topic:

It is recorded in the Koran that Prophet Mohamed was 40 years old when he was elevated to the station of prophethood. It is also narrated in hadith that Mohamed "said that a human being stays in his mother's womb 40 days in the form of a sperm (*nutfah*), for 40 days in the form of clot (*alaqah*) and for forty days in the form of a shapeless lump (*mudghghah*)." Then God sends an angel to breathe the soul into him.

While we may differ on theological lines especially as to when life begins, and we will leave that for another day, the significance of the number 40 interests us at this juncture.

Folks, as stated earlier, the number forty is mentioned 146 times in Scripture, and its significance in both the Old and New Testaments cannot be overemphasized. It is on this basis, especially in regard to my dear country, Liberia, that we are for the most part bringing this revelation.

It is my hope that because of the significance of the mysterious number 40, across religious, spiritual, cultural, and traditional backgrounds, all of us as a nation, regardless of religious, political, ethnic, and traditional persuasions, will join forces and embrace the shifting that is hovering over the nation.

THE SIGNIFICANCE OF THE SEASON

"There is a time for everything, and a season for every activity under the heavens."

ECCLESIASTES 3:1 NIV

This verse of Scripture speaks to the importance of times and seasons. For every activity on the earth, there is a season. When we look at the creation of the universe itself, we realize that God is the God of order and season as He made everything beautiful in accordance with its own time and season. God could have made everything in one day at a single declaration. Of course, His omnipotence allows for that, but He created the heavens and the earth in an orderly fashion.

God, in His creation of the earth, did not send rain until there was man to till the ground:

"And every plant of the field before it was in the earth, and every herb of the field before it grew: for the Lord God had not caused it to rain upon the earth, and there was not a man to till the ground."

GENESIS 2:5 KJV

It is amazing how the Almighty held the rain for a season and waited for the right season to release it.

If God, creator of seasons, values the principles of timing and season, who are we, His creatures, not to? We are supposed to be men and women who yearn to understand the times and seasons and act accordingly for the realization of visions.

Many dreams and visions have been prematurely aborted

because the visionary did not attach value to timing and season. When your season is at hand, and you do not seize the opportunity, you have missed a glorious opportunity to actualize your dream.

When Jesus was born in Bethlehem, the first persons who knew about it were magi, if you like, the wise men, who saw the star and knew exactly that it heralded the season for the king of the Jews to be born.

Seasons are accompanied by signs. God may not come and speak to you in an audible voice but God speaks and shows Himself through signs. When such signs are revealed, it is left with us to seize the opportunity.

In the context of a call for national shifting, it is very clear that we are in our 40s from 1980 when all hell broke loose. We are now in the peak season as we head into an election when a decision needs to be made to either place the nation on the right trajectory for a positive shifting or we decide to further retrogress and remain the poorest or one of the poorest nations in the world!

When the wise men saw the sign, they acted by moving right away. Even though they didn't know the exact place where the king was born, they took off. They didn't sit there wondering as to the whereabouts of the newborn king. They took off immediately. Today, they are part of history. Generations after generations read and talk about the magi whose bravery led them to the king, who would have had them killed just by inquiring of the birth of the new king. However, they braved the storm and acted. Eventually, they finally realized their dream of meeting the newborn king.

Folks, let us take a moment to underscore the significance that the wise men attached to the season of Jesus' birth. Most times, as we read this verse, we don't highlight this aspect. However, in the context of national shifting, it takes complete bravery to cause a shift and to act accordingly.

Only people who are bold as lions can do this. The wise men would have been killed immediately as their quest to even find the new king was tantamount to undermining the kingship of Herod. But they didn't mind; they asked the hard questions, and Herod heard it. Wow! The bravery of the wise men cannot be overemphasized owing to the absolute power that monarchs of ancient days had.

In our next chapter, we will focus on acting on the times and seasons which is very critical because we can attach all the significance to the season but if we don't seize the season, there can be no shifting.

CHAPTER FIVE

Seizing The Season

"And the children of Issachar, which were men that had understanding of the times, to know what Israel ought to do."

1 CHRONICLES 12:32A NIV

In this final chapter, our attention will be on the latter phrase in 1 Chronicles 12:32b which says, *"to know what Israel ought to do."* The men of Issachar didn't just have an understanding of the times and seasons, but they knew exactly what to do to cause a shift, and this will be the basis of our discussion throughout this chapter.

We can have all the faith and engage in all kinds of prayers and prophetic declarations about shifting, but if we don't act and seize the season, we aren't going anywhere.

Scripture declares that faith without works is dead:

"As the body without the spirit is dead, so faith without deed is dead."

JAMES 2:26 NIV

So much faith for shifting has been released. Our churches are full of prayer warriors praying day and night for shifting. Yet, from time to time, we remain in the same position and, don't get me wrong, prayer is very essential in the shifting process; however, there is something fundamentally missing. I love the way Bishop Tudor Bismark puts it: "Prayer is not in the success equation; prayer is in the revelation equation; decision-making is in the success equation."

Whilst we are praying, declaring, and releasing all the faith for a shifting, we also need to get involved in the decision-making. Gone are the days when we sat on the fence and left national decision-making with wicked and feeble-minded people.

VEHICLE FOR THE SHIFTING

As we talk about the decision-making process in this chapter, our goal is to clearly define the vehicle for the shifting process and that simply means those that are supposed to get involved and trigger the shifting.

I love this quote from the book, *What God Looks for in His Vessel*, "The scarcity of the wonders of God in any generation is not the deficiency of God in that generation but the unavailability of usable men." This is powerful!

The wonder of shifting in our nations will not happen until usable and humble men and women make themselves available to be used for this shifting process, and that decision must be made by us.

Let me begin by saying the shifting of the country is solely dependent on all of us as a nation, young and old, irrespective of our religious and ethnic orientations. However, I'd like to call out the Church of Jesus Christ, as I believe we are supposed to be the champion of this shifting movement. It will interest you to know that Scripture declares:

> *"For unto us a child is born, to us a son is given, and the government shall be upon his shoulders. And He will be called wonderful counselor, mighty God, everlasting father, prince of peace."*
>
> ISAIAH 9:6 NIV

The statement I'd like to draw your attention to in this verse is, "and the government shall be upon his shoulders". This is a clear indication that the Church, the body of Christ, is a carrier of the government. Judging from this Scripture, the Church is supposed to be the enabler and the source of power.

However, you don't need a rocket scientist to tell you that, ironically, in this day and age, the government has become the carrier of the Church on its shoulders as some elders at the gate and fathers in the land have belittled themselves for little or nothing. Some of the bids and tactics that politicians have used to trap our fathers are money and the offer of lucrative government jobs. Once they fall into the bid and traps, their advocacy and messages change, and they join the wagon of sycophancy and flattery. What a pity; we certainly need a shifting!

In the 2000s after the civil war, there was a bishop who became a lawmaker. One day, he went on the media and publicly criticized his colleagues for the ills that were in that body, and he was very vocal and critical, but his criticism lasted for a few days as his fellow lawmakers threatened to vote for his suspension and denial of salary and immunities if he didn't retract his criticism. It wasn't long and the next day, he was on radio, walking back every word he uttered the previous day.

In fact, in his speech, this is what he said: "the devil hijacked that sermon," and he appealed to his colleagues for forgiveness. What a pity that was!

Meanwhile, those who do not fall prey to the temptation of money and lucrative jobs are often reduced to simply praying and making prophetic declarations for the nation. Listen, national shifting is not merely dependent on prophecy; it requires firm and concrete actions.

It is high time the church rises above sycophancy, laziness, and passivity. "Prayer is not in the success equation but the revelation equation; decision-making is in the success equation," and now is the time for action.

Let me also indicate that whilst we are critical of the role of men of God being involved in matters of governance, I want to make it clear that there is no problem with a man of God who feels called to serve in government to be involved in governance as long as they have that calling. In fact, if it is not us, the children of light, then who?

However, there has to be clear evidence of the call of God in that area like Daniel, Nehemiah, and others who, even though were prophets of God, served in the government of their days with distinction. Daniel was considered a man of excellent spirit:

"Then this Daniel was preferred above all the presidents and princes, because an excellent spirit was found in him; and the King thought to set him over the whole realm."

DANIEL 6:3 KJV

It is indeed highly recommended that children of light with the calling and the spirit of excellence rise up to serve in government, but when the calling is not there and one is only going into a governmental role because of the money, prestige, and power that come along, it becomes a disaster, and this is what we have seen repeatedly.

As a prophet in the land, I am using this medium to rally the church to stand up because we are that vehicle that God wants to use to usher in the necessary shifting. If we don't stand up in this season and do what is necessary for the shifting, our nation will continue in its misery and backwardness, and history will not be kind to us.

GOD'S STANDARDS FOR NATIONAL LEADERSHIP

Because everything rises and falls on leadership, and our numerous problems as a nation are often due to bad leadership, it is my hope this section will go a long way to help you discover the standards set by God for those who step into national leadership. Just as I mentioned elsewhere in this book, a problem discovered is a problem nearly solved. It is my prayer that this discovery will open the eyes of your understanding in choosing your national leaders.

To begin with, let me debunk a common saying used by pastors, politicians, and ordinary people: "The voice of the people is the voice of God." How sad it is that one would think that the voice of a majority will always be consistent with God's voice. It doesn't matter how many billions of voices speak in one voice to a particular situation; the voice of God is unique and superintends over every other voice. And so, I'd like to state categorically that the voice of the people may at times align with, but is never in and of itself the voice of God. This is what God said to Isaiah:

"For my thoughts are not your thoughts, neither are your ways my ways, declares the Lord, as the heavens are higher than the earth, so are my ways higher than your ways and my thoughts than your thoughts."

ISAIAH 55:8-9 NIV

Scripture is filled with examples of the voice of the people being in complete opposition to the voice of God. The voice and will of the people would have led them back to Egypt under Moses and Israel rejected God as their King under Samuel to mention just a few.

Listen to this:

"Then all of the elders of Israel gathered themselves together, and came to Samuel unto Ramma, and said unto him behold thy art old, and thy sons walk not in thy ways: now make us a king to judge us like all the nations. But the thing displeased Samuel when they said give us a king to judge us. And Samuel prayed unto the Lord. And the Lord said unto Samuel, harken unto the voice of the people in all that they say unto thee: for they have not rejected thee, but they have rejected me, that I should not

reign over them."

1 SAMUEL 8:4-7 KJV

This is a clear example of the fallacy of the "voice of the people is the voice of God,".

As humans, we are prone to errors, so in every election cycle, we make bad decisions and choose the wrong leaders. This is simply because God doesn't approve, in most cases, of our chosen leaders.

As we discuss God's standard for national leadership, let us talk about the three Cs that God has laid on my heart. When we say the 3 Cs, we are talking about *Calling, Character,* and *Charisma;* these are very important in our quest to identify God's stamped and approved leaders.

Let's talk about the calling, which is the very foundation on which national leadership must be rooted.

 CALLING

The calling speaks to the fact that leaders must be called by God, singled out, and predestined to serve on the national level. As we see clearly in Scripture, God called leaders to serve Israel in certain seasons. Leaders called by God have the fire and passion in them to serve, as they aren't in service because of fame and money.

God said to Jeremiah about his calling:

"Before I formed you in the womb, I knew you, before you

67

were born, I set you apart; I appointed you as a prophet to the nations."

Inasmuch as this Scripture may specifically refer to the calling of Jeremiah's prophetic ministry to the nations, the same principles apply to national political leadership as it is seen, for example, in the case of King Saul even though Samuel, God's representative who led Israel, was rejected by the Israelites. God still had a role in whom became the next king.

This is what God said to Samuel concerning Saul:

"Now the day before Saul came, the Lord had revealed this to Samuel: 'About this time tomorrow I will send you a man from the land of Benjamin. Anoint him ruler over my people Israel; he will deliver them from the hand of the Philistines. I have looked on my people, for their cry has reached me.' When Samuel caught site of Saul, the Lord said to him, 'this is the man I spoke to you about; he will govern my people.'"

1 SAMUEL 9:15-17 NIV

It is crystal clear in this Scripture that even though Samuel and God weren't the happiest as a result of Israel's rejection of God as their chosen King, yet God was still involved in the process of determining who became their king. Saul was called by God to serve for that season.

The calling is very critical even beyond national leadership. Many miss out on their true callings and vocations and are misplaced, thereby circumventing destinies. It is high time we watch out for those who are truly called to national leadership, and we will know them by their fruits.

CHARACTER

Leaders are called, and character is developed, just like Moses was called by God from birth to be the deliverer of Israel from Egyptian slavery. This is seen as the Lord spared his life from death when all Jewish boys were being murdered at the orders of the very Pharaoh who raised him up.

Moses was truly called as a leader, but he needed some major character development to qualify him in accordance with God's standards. Moses may have gotten all the exposure and the best education whilst being raised in Pharaoh's house as an adopted son (tradition has it that this Pharaoh did not have a boy child save for his daughter's adopted son). This meant that Moses was a direct heir to the Egyptian Pharaoh.

However, God has His own standards for leadership, which are different from the world's. Thus, He took Moses from Egypt to Midian for forty good years, as we learned earlier, humbled him and gave him the right character to lead Israel out of slavery.

So, in this section, our goal is to lay out those standards set by God for His called leaders so we ensure that those assuming national leadership are judged by them because, personal character is critical to national leadership.

FAITH

"The fear of the Lord is the beginning of wisdom."

PROVERBS 9:10A KJV

This passage of Scripture clearly indicates that whilst wisdom is the principal thing, and it is the source of power and wealth, there is something much better than wisdom and that's a relationship with God. The fear of the Lord, which connotes a right standing with God is certainly a very important qualification for national leadership.

Most times, we care less about the faith of our leaders, and that's a big mistake that often backfires. The faith of our leaders must be checked properly.

From a Christian perspective, we should be concerned about a national leader's genuine relationship with God. Is he or she genuinely born-again and part of an assembly where he or she is growing in fellowship with the Holy Spirit? Being a part of an assembly is very important, as Paul warns against forsaking the assembly of the brethren.

"Not forsaken our meeting together as is the habit of some, but encouraging one another, and all the more as you see the day of Christ's return approaching."

HEBREWS 10:25 AMP

FAMILY

The significance of the family life of a leader cannot be overemphasized, as there is a lot of Scriptural backing for this qualification. When he ran away from Egypt while in his processing period, Moses settled his family status as he got married in exile before returning to undertake the massive task of leading

Israel out of Egypt. This means that it was all part of God's plan to prepare Moses for the massive task.

I am not intimating that one must be married before taking on a national leadership role, but it is very important that leaders at the helm of national leadership must be faithful to their wives and family as a whole. The 1 Timothy 3 qualifications for church leadership are very essential and can be applied to national leadership.

This is what Paul says:

"Now the overseer is to be above reproach, faithful to his wife."

1 TIMOTHY 3:2 NIV

He goes further by saying:

"He must manage his own family well and see that his children obey him, and he must do so in a manner worthy of full respect. If anyone does not know how to manage his own family, how can he take care of God's church?"

1 TIMOTHY 3:4 NIV

While these passages may be in the context of an overseer of a church, the principles transcend the church setting as they apply to oversee a nation.

Those serving in national leadership must have a good family background; the married must be faithful to his wife and not parading with girlfriends all over the place. In fact, some go as far as having extramarital affairs and having children outside of their marital relationships. Sadly, society has become comfortable with it. What a shame!

Paul goes further by raising the bar that the leader must manage his family well, ensuring that his children obey him and are under his control. If a leader cannot manage his family, how can he manage a nation? This qualification is often downplayed, and for the most part, those who end up being victims are the same people who hail morally bankrupt leaders. They make statements to the effect that whatever a leader chooses to do in his or her private life has nothing to do with their public service. Shame on you if you thought so or acted this way. It's time to shift.

HONESTY

Honesty is a very significant characteristic of national leadership. Earlier, when we looked at the principle of us being the source of our own problems, we highlighted dishonesty and corruption as key reasons why our country remains impoverished and underdeveloped. In Proverbs, the writer says this about honesty:

> *"Whoever walks in integrity walks securely, but whoever takes crooked paths will be found out."*
> PROVERBS 10:9 NIV

Here, integrity connotes honesty; meaning, when you are an honest person, you are secure in this life, but dishonesty brings many troubles, not only to the dishonest individual who is eventually found out, but to his surroundings as there is a ripple effect.

An honest person is more concerned about his or her legacy than the attainment of wealth.

"A good name is more desirable than great riches; to be esteemed is better than silver or gold."

PROVERBS 22:1 NIV

In my lifetime, I have seen people who rose to national leadership and, by their action and inactions, destroy the name of their families; I mean, generations after them will suffer the effect of their dishonesty.

What is also troubling is that I have seen that there is a portion of society that encourages and embraces dishonesty; so, when a man gets a job in the public sector or wherever, especially a job with a big portfolio and lives squarely on his salary and is not concerned about taking bribes and cutting corners and stealing to buy a comfortable car, build a big house or travel, etc. like some do, he or she is considered a *mumu* (fool).

Dishonesty is a cancer spreading like wildfire, eating up the nation's wealth. It is high time that honest men and women rise to power, challenge the status quo, and make a difference.

HUMILITY

A leader's humility is a very significant trait in assuming national leadership as it is clearly indicated in Scriptures that: "God opposes the proud but shows favor to the humble". In this sinful and perverse world where the temptation of pride and arrogance looms over leadership in every aspect of society, it takes humble leadership to thrive.

Society is structured so that leaders easily succumb to the temptation of pride and excessive power. Sometimes, it is the followers who push leaders into being very powerful and arrogant, but you and I know that the same people will complain about the pride and arrogance of a leader someday. Never give in to it, your way up is down, my friend.

Jesus set a perfect example for us whilst on his earthly ministry. One day at a supper he shocked his followers when he did an unusual thing to set the stage for humble and servant leadership. The Master, Jesus took a towel and began to wash his disciples' feet. One of them, Peter, was so shocked that he refused to be washed. The rest of the story in John 13 speaks for itself. If followed, the simplicity of leadership as portrayed by Jesus will shift society forever. Imagine the creator and owner of the earth who cared less about the luxury and power of this world to the extent that he borrowed a donkey to ride in Jerusalem.

How many of our national leaders today will choose to lay pride aside and do away with luxury that comes with leadership? Even for a poor country like ours, our national leaders will choose pride, excess, and luxury at the detriment of the poor. They ride in expensive cars, which they change every other year.

They fly around the world in private jets, and build massive mansions for themselves overnight, mansions they cannot manage in a few years when they are out of power. How much does one need to be satisfied? At any point in time, you can only sleep in one house, one room, and on one bed. In fact, on that bed, sadly, it is just one comfortable spot and a pillow, but they plunder wealth of the nation, leaving the rest of the country in abject poverty. It's time for shifting.

EMPATHY

Let us talk about the empathy of a leader as a very important trait in assuming national leadership. The simplest definition of empathy, from my perspective, will be putting your feet in another person's shoes. I think a leader should be one who understands exactly what his followers or those he leads are going through and identifies with them.

This is what Paul said to the church in Rome:

> *"Be happy with those who are happy and weep with those who weep."*
>
> ROMANS 12:15 NIV

Whilst Paul is speaking generally to every Christian. This trait is even more applicable to leaders who are supposed to be an example to those they lead. Scripture declares that to whom much is given, much is required.

We see national leaders easily become heartless as they rise to national leadership. In fact, during campaign periods, they come like angels as they identify with everyone in nearly everything, but deep in their hearts, they are fooling around only to rise to power. Once they achieve their goals of becoming leaders, they are done. This is a very common experience in politics, and that's why electorates in every election cycle vote out nearly all elected officials because they feel betrayed.

Here is the solution: with this guide, we can begin to hold leaders accountable before they rise to leadership by checking them out if they truly have these traits before vying for national leadership. Be-ware of overnight humanitarians; they are often wolves in sheep's clothing.

DISCIPLINE

A leader's discipline cannot be overemphasized as it is a fundamental trait for those assuming national leadership. First, let's look at what Scripture says about the significance of leadership discipline.

> *"Whoever heeds discipline shows the way to life, but whoever ignores correction leads others astray."*
>
> PROVERBS 10:17 NIV

To be disciplined means that one obeys rules and instructions. In the passage highlighted, the writer clearly is speaking of someone in a leadership position who heeds instruction and is on the path to success in life. On the contrary, he leads others astray if he doesn't follow instructions or walks in maturity.

Nowadays, there is a serious deficit in discipline among leaders. It is sad to say that indiscipline is the order of the day. Leaders are supposed to be role models in society. This means they should be an example by following and obeying the rules so that others follow. However, the contrary is what is real. In most cases, lawmakers are usually the law-breakers. The integrity to uphold the rule of law is lacking. When leadership lacks the moral standing to enforce discipline like the rule of law, society chaotic. It is high time we watch out for the disciplinary traits of those aspiring to be in positions of national leadership.

INTEGRITY

Earlier, we looked at honesty, a sub-trait of integrity, which we singled out because of its significance in leadership as we thought to do a more detailed discussion of it.

However, this section will look at the generality of moral integrity as a significant godly standard for national leadership. One of the major problems societies face today in leadership is the issue of moral bankruptcy. The breakdown of moral integrity in leadership is a root cause of the many problems we are having in our society because a massive percentage of today's national leaders do not have the moral standing to champion morality and bring moral order to our institutions. However, this is not unique to national leaders, but a ripple effect in all aspects of society, and this has to be addressed.

Before we go further, let's look at what Scripture says about integrity:

"The integrity of the upright guides them, but the unfaithful are destroyed by their duplicity."

PROVERBS 11:3 NIV

This passage of Scripture makes it very plain that the upright will be guided by integrity, which means that in the midst of a world in where moral-defensive walls are broken, infiltrated, and permeated by moral bankruptcy, we can be certain that with integrity, we can be guided, and, eventually, succeed in our leadership journey.

The other side of the coin is leaders who choose the other way around, as the Scripture puts it are destroyed by their duplicity, which speaks to their deceitful and double-dealing style of leadership.

One thing that is clear in this passage is that moral bankruptcy leads to destruction. Meanwhile, it is important to note that the destruction mentioned is not just for the unfaithful leader, but there is a collateral damage that society faces when morality breaks down. When leaders mess up, the effect is not only for the leader, but we all face the consequences. That is why it is very important that we put into leadership individuals whose personal character is in line with God's standards for national leadership because personal character is critical to leadership.

When people are deceitful, untruthful, hateful, cheaters, unstable, dishonest, promiscuous, and divisive, we cannot say it is a personal or private matter. When they stand up for national leadership, they should be judged by the content of those characteristics. If we allow the contrary, we become hypocritical, particularly for those who are the children of God. It is high time we call a spade a spade and put away our personal interests and put God's interest first. Secondly, the interest of the nation should come before our personal interests. When we do this, society will shift for good.

VISION

Visionary leadership in national leadership cannot be overstressed because most of the problems we have faced over the years as a nation are not just the breakdown of morality but the lack of vision.

The Bible says something about that;

> *"Where there is no vision the people perish: but he that keepeth the law, happy is he."*
>
> PROVERB 29:18 KJV

As revealed by Scripture, it is clear that lack of vision in national leadership leads to the breakdown of national development, as it takes leaders who are concerned about tomorrow and not just today. It takes farsighted leaders, not short-sighted leaders, to build for the future.

Nations ahead in development are those whose leaders were visionaries as they looked into the future and invested time and resources. A nation whose leaders are shortsighted and self-centered is not concerned about the future of the country. The result of that is doom, just as the Scripture declares: "people perish" because of the lack of vision.

Meanwhile, it is important that leaders who rise to national leadership are leaders with vision. How do you know them? It is by their fruits. Watch out for visionary leaders.

PASSION

As we conclude on our second C being Character, it is important that we highlight a very a critical characteristic which is drawn out of vision. This is passion. A truly visionary leader is a passionate leader. Without passion, a vision cannot be realized. Passion is the fire that drives the implementation and realization of vision, and every visionary leader needs that fire.

The richest place on planet earth is not the diamond mines of South Africa, or the oil-rich soils of Kuwait or Saudi Arabia; the richest place on planet earth is the cemeteries where people with massive visions and dreams never realized in their lifetime lie. This failure is, in most cases, due to the lack of passion that led to the failure of those visionaries to bring their visions to pass.

Listen to what Scripture says about passion:

"Whatever your hands find to do, do it with all your might, for in the realm of the dead, where you are going, there is neither working nor planning nor knowledge nor wisdom."

ECCLESIASTES 9:10 NIV

So, it is clear that whatever your hands find to do, do it with all your might, and all your might connotes passion which is the fire that powers your vision and dreams into realization. Early on, we talked about the richest place on earth being the cemeteries and not our perceived rich places. In this passage of Scripture, we are reminded that there is no work or planning in the grave where we will all end up. It means that as leaders, we have to work passionately.

CHARISMA

"That the servant of God may be thoroughly equipped for every good work."

2 TIMOTHY 3:17 NIV

After detailing our second C, which is Character, in this session, our goal is to look at the third and final C under God's standards for national leadership which speaks to the Charisma of the leader. It is interesting to note that in most cases, especially in the secular world, when a leader is being sought or qualified, most times, what tops the list of criteria for qualification is charisma which has to do with the special personal quality or power of an individual making him or her capable of influencing or inspiring larger numbers of people.

In addition to what charisma is, it is derived from the Greek word meaning favor or gift. In fact, charisma was originally used in a Christian context to refer to a gift or power bestowed upon an individual by the Holy Spirit.

So, in the context of national leadership, we will look at those personal qualities that an individual needs to have in order to assume national leadership.

GIFTINGS

Let's begin by considering gifting as a very important aspect of assuming national leadership. Leaders endowed with leadership skills perform exceedingly better than those picked by chance and thrust into positions of power. It is a disaster for someone without leadership abilities to serve in leadership. Some people are just followers, and if they become national leaders, they plunge the country and its people into a mess. Gifted leaders are known by their fruits.

A perfect example is David, who became king of Israel. As a young man, David took good care of his father's sheep. He provided effective leadership because he was a gifted leader. Listen to what David said when he stood before Saul on a day when Israel desperately needed a leader to defeat Goliath:

> *"But David said to Saul 'your servant has been keeping his father's sheep. When a lion came or a bear came and carried off a sheep from the flock, I went after it, stuck it and rescued the sheep from its mouth. When it turned on me, I seized it by its hair struck it and kill it.'"*
>
> 1 SAMUEL 17:34-35 NIV

In this Scripture, we see a full display of a gifted leader as David assures Saul that by the help of God, he was capable of defeating Goliath based on the leadership ability that God had given him. Dr. Myles Munroe once said, "An army of sheep led by a lion will always defeat an army of lions led by a sheep."

In essence, this speaks to the quality that gifted leadership brings to the table. Gifted leaders get the job done effectively. It is high time we watch out for leaders with the ability to lead as opposed to risking our future and children's future with people who are mere followers.

EXPERIENCE

Let us look at experience as a very important standard under the caption of charisma in our drive to set godly standards for national leadership. One may be a gifted leader, but once you have not exercised that gift in any way, shape, or form, it becomes difficult to effectively administer your leadership ability.

It is important to note that the gifted and greatest leaders in biblical times had their own experiences and preparation before assuming the leadership role that God destined them for. Earlier, we talked about David when we discussed giftings. David was highly gifted and skilled by God, but he needed to be processed before assuming the role of a king. At a very young age, he was trusted with the responsibility of taking care of sheep, and that was a learning experience. He effectively provided for and protected the sheep. Moving forward, he killed Goliath. In fact, God took him to Saul's palace because of his musical gifting; there, he learned about royalty as well.

Let's take a look at this Scripture:

"And Saul said unto his servants, provide me now a man that can play well, and bring him to me. Then answered one of the servants, and said, behold, I have seen a son of Jesse the Bethlehemite, that is cunning in playing, and a mighty valiant man, and a man of war, and prudent in matters, and a comely person, and the Lord is with him. Wherefore, Saul sent messengers unto Jesse, and said, send me David thy son, which is with the sheep. And David came to Saul, and stood before: and he loved him greatly; and he became his armor bearer."

1 SAMUEL 16:17-21 KJV

Let's take a look at Moses; he was one of the greatest leaders of biblical times as he was called by God to lead Israel out of slavery to the Promised Land. Even though he was a gifted leader, God took him through a learning curve. First, in the palace, where he got the elite educational experience of his time. You see, educational experience is very critical to national leadership, and sometimes, this is overlooked. We thereby put people with little or no educational experience in leadership and the result can be disastrous.

Moses' leadership experience didn't end in the palace. He was taken to the desert of Midian, where he lived under harsh conditions, taking care of sheep and raising a family for forty unbroken years before returning to Egypt to provide leadership for Israel.

Now you can see clearly how these great and successful leaders of their time, even though called and gifted by God, needed a great deal of experience and processing to fulfill God's call on their lives.

Today, we bring to national leadership inexperienced and irresponsible neophytes with the hope that they will learn on the job. God doesn't guarantee that; He is the God of principles, protocols, and order.

As we conclude on God's standards for national leadership, I wish to remind you that national leadership is a very critical and delicate area that all need serious attention. Hence, our decision to choose leaders should be well-thought through. It is my hope that these standards will help the ordinary masses of our nation and nations around the world in bringing into national leadership credible candidates that will ultimately transform our nation and global village.

Conclusion

As we conclude this book, I would like to thank you for taking the time to read through this prophetic call for national shifting. It is my hope that you will heed this call and be a part of the shifting process that's happening in your nation.

In these end-times, it is the plan of God to bring in the earth His Kingdom, where governments of the world are led by individuals who submit to His will and promote His Kingdom agenda. Because democracy gives people the power to choose leaders, we play a pivotal role in His shifting process, as the right to choose is in our hands.

In Jesus' famous prayer, this is what he taught us to pray:

> *"Your kingdom come, your will be done on earth as it is in heaven."*

MATTHEW 6:10 NIV

It is important to note that while democracy is hailed and preached as the best system of governance of our day, let me express that democracy in itself is not perfect as we clearly can see that from time to time because of our human limitations and imperfections. We fall short in choosing the right people for national leadership.

God says:

"For my thoughts are not your thoughts, neither are your ways my ways declares the Lord."

ISAIAH 55:8 NIV

This passage of Scripture clearly underscores the need to depend on God in our decision much more so in choosing our leaders, because leadership makes or breaks organizations and nations. If a nation will prosper, it will surely depend on the leadership that is in place. You might have heard the saying, "Everything rises and falls on leadership."

Listen to this:

"When the righteous are in authority, the people rejoice: but when the wicked beareth rule, the people mourn."

PROVERBS 29:2 KJV

This Scripture speaks to the significance of the righteous being in power, leading to a happy nation. The word rejoice in the passage speaks to blessings, prosperity and peace. A nation that has God-fearing leaders in authority will enjoy the blessings and peace of God, but with the wicked continuously in power, our global village will continue to see wars, destruction, and economic collapse. We can never get better unless we shift and allow the will of God and the Kingdom of God to prevail in our national leadership.

Meanwhile, my hope and prayer is that this book will prove a helpful tool in the process of God bringing a shifting and the power He has placed in your hands. Most times we Christians shy away from political processes which leads to bringing into power wicked and corrupt leaders. In the end, we all suffer the consequences of those bad decisions. I hope this book fires you up to rise up and do the right thing by getting involved in these processes by going out to vote for leaders who meet the standards of God as laid out in this book.

As I conclude, I would like to speak specifically to the people of my dearest nation, Liberia; it is the 40th season from 1980 when all hell broke loose in this country.

Folks, as we go to elections this year, I need you to pray first about your choice or choices of leaders. As you know, prayer is very critical in this process. Secondly, you have been provided with the tools you need to determine who becomes a national leader, and this is not just for the presidency and vice presidency but the entire legislature. I'm talking about senators and representatives.

The election of every national leader is critical. Sometimes our attention is focused on the presidency, and we forget that lawmakers are the lieutenants of the people and should have oversight, and in most cases, they are not properly vetted. They even buy your votes in some cases. Listen, it is time for a paradigm shift. Encourage yourself, mobilize your family, your church, your community, and let the nation rise up and do the right thing by voting in these elections and every election cycle.

ABOUT THE AUTHOR

David Saa Fatorma, Jr. is the General Overseer of the Light Streams Chapel Solution Outreach Ministries. He is married to Veronica, and they are blessed with five children. He has planted several churches across the nation of Liberia and leads few church networks.

He is a media personality as he broadcasts the Word of God on several radio stations across Liberia weekly. He also runs teaching programs on TV, notable New Day Hour Sunday morning teachings and Voice of the Church that discusses socio-political, economic, religious, and trending national issues from an unbiased and biblical perspective. He holds a Master's Degree in Theology and has traveled in several countries across the world preaching the Gospel of Jesus Christ.

David Fatorma is a survivor of a massacre which happened during the 15-year civil war in Liberia and has authored a book which details his survival through the miraculous intervention of God.

ABOUT THE BOOK

The necessity for national shifting in our global village cannot be overemphasized as there is an urgent need for a shifting for restoring sanity, normalcy, and enhancing God's will and kingdom agenda in our governments.

This book provides details on a prophetic call for national shifting with specific reference to Liberia, a nation in its prophetic season of shifting. Overall, this book reminds God's children of their role in enhancing the shifting of our nations and provides a clear guide for that process.

www.ingramcontent.com/pod-product-compliance
Lightning Source LLC
Chambersburg PA
CBHW070441130626
46553CB00006B/2270